# Raaz-O-Niyaaz

मेरे दिल के कुछ हसीन हिस्से
और कुछ प्यारे मुँह ज़बानी क़िस्से

Siddharth Thakkar

India | USA | UK

Copyright © Siddharth Thakkar
All Rights Reserved.

This book has been self-published with all reasonable efforts taken to make the material error-free by the author. No part of this book shall be used, reproduced in any manner whatsoever without written permission from the author, except in the case of brief quotations embodied in critical articles and reviews.

The Author of this book is solely responsible and liable for its content including but not limited to the views, representations, descriptions, statements, information, opinions, and references ["Content"]. The Content of this book shall not constitute or be construed or deemed to reflect the opinion or expression of the Publisher or Editor. Neither the Publisher nor Editor endorse or approve the Content of this book or guarantee the reliability, accuracy, or completeness of the Content published herein and do not make any representations or warranties of any kind, express or implied, including but not limited to the implied warranties of merchantability, fitness for a particular purpose.

The Publisher and Editor shall not be liable whatsoever...

Made with ❤ on the BookLeaf Publishing Platform
www.bookleafpub.in
www.bookleafpub.com

# Dedication

उस प्रेम के नाम—
जो थमा नहीं,
बल्कि वह जो बिछड़ कर भी अमर रहने की ज़िद ठाने रहा।

उस अहसास को
जो एक मुकम्मल दास्तान न बन सका,
किन्तु इस पुस्तक का हर नज़्म, हर मिसरा बन गया।

उस गहरी, शांत कसक को
जो लोगों के गुज़र जाने के बाद भी
एक टीस बनकर दिल में बसी रही।
क्योंकि, अंततः, इसी ख़ामोशी ने
इन शब्दों को मुझ तक पहुँचाया।

To love—
not the kind that lasted,
but the kind that left and still refused to die.

To what couldn't become a story,
yet became every verse in this book.

To the quiet ache that stayed
long after the people didn't.
For it was in that silence
that these words found me.

# Preface

ये कविताएँ किसी इरादे से नहीं रची गईं,
बल्कि महसूस की गईं—एक टीस, एक याद, एक मौसम के क्रम में।

कुछ प्रेम की ऊष्मा से उपजीं;
कुछ उसके चले जाने के बाद की ठंडक से निकलीं।
ये सब मिलकर एक हृदय की धीमी यात्रा को दर्शाती हैं—
समर्पण से विरक्ति की ओर, थामे रखने से समझ जाने की ओर।

हर कविता उस क्षण का प्रतिबिंब है जो कभी अनंत-सा लगा था।
ये पंक्तियाँ किसी एक को समर्पित नहीं हैं,
फिर भी उन सबकी हैं जिन्होंने कभी प्रेम किया, खोया, और यह सीखा
कि अंत भी सुंदर हो सकते हैं जब वे आपको जीना और महसूस करना सिखाते हैं।

अगर इस संग्रह में कोई सूत्र है जो सबको पिरोता है,
तो वह यही है कि प्रेम—चाहे वह वर्तमान हो या अतीत—
ईश्वर से मिलने का सबसे मानवीय माध्यम है।

These poems were not written with intent,
but felt—one ache, one memory, one season at a time.

Some came from the warmth of love;
some from the chill that follows its leaving.
Together, they trace the slow journey of a heart—
from devotion to detachment, from holding on to understanding.

Each poem stands as a reflection of a moment that once felt infinite.
They are not addressed to anyone,
yet belong to everyone who has ever loved, lost, and learned
that even endings can be beautiful when they teach you to feel.

If there is a thread running through this collection,
it is that love—whether present or past—
remains the most human way to meet the divine.

# Acknowledgements

उन लोगों के लिए जिन्होंने मुझमें वह गहरा एहसास जगाया कि मैं लिख सका।

शायद आप कभी न जानें कि ये पन्ने अंशतः आपके ही हैं,
पर आपकी उपस्थिति ने—चाहे कितनी भी क्षणिक रही हो—मेरे शब्दों को धड़कन दी।

उन सबको जो जीवन में आए, साथ ठहरे, चले गए, या अब तक दिल में बने हुए हैं—आपका धन्यवाद।
आपने साधारण पलों को यादगार बनाया,
और उन यादों को जीवन का अर्थ दिया।

समय के नाम—मुझे सिखाने के लिए कि हर टूटी हुई चीज़ को जोड़ना आवश्यक नहीं होता।
और स्वयं प्रेम के नाम—उस अनमोल शेष के लिए, जो बिछड़ने के बाद भी शेष रहा।

To the people who once made me feel deeply enough to write.
You may never know these pages are partly yours,
but your presence—however brief—gave my words their heartbeat.

To those who came, stayed, left, or lingered—thank you.
You turned ordinary moments into memories,
and memories into meaning.

To time—for teaching me that not everything broken needs to be fixed.
And to love itself—for leaving behind what even absence couldn't take away.

# तलाश-ए-खुदा

बीत जाती है उमरें
ना जाने किस की तलाश में
तू इंसान है या इश्क-ए-खुदा
जो तू मिले सिर्फ़ अरदास में
होगा ये नसीबो का ही कुछ खेल
मिलने को मिल जाती है खैरात में


A lifetime passes by
Searching for someone/something unknown.
Are you a human, or the love of God ?
That is only found in sincere prayer
Perhaps this is just a trick of fate!
That one can find the desired meeting in mere charity/alms

# इस्तीफ़ा-ए-इश्क

इम्तेहानो की इंतहा हो गई
एक नज़र में उमरें वफ़ा हो गई
यूं मैं दिखने में ही जिंदा हूं बस
अब मुझे दफना दो यारो
वो नाजनीन कब की बेवफा हो गई


The limit of all trials and tests has been reached,
A lifetime of loyalty was pledged in a single glance.
I am merely alive in appearance, that's all.
Now, friends, just bury me,
That my delicate beauty became unfaithful long ago.

# इश्क-ए-खुदा

जो तू छू के ऐसा निकला है
शायद खुदा का कोई अज़ीज़ हूं मैं
जिस प्यार की मिसाल दे दुनिया
उस रब्बानी रब की मूरत तुझमें
तू पूरा दिल है मेरा
तू कोई हिस्सा नहीं जो अलग झूमे
तू मिलना मुझे फिर उसी जगह
जहाँ ज़मीन को फ़लक चूमे

The way you have emerged, having touched me,
Perhaps I am someone dear to God.
The world gives an example of the love you embody,
You are the image of that divine Lord .
You are my complete heart,
You are not a part that could sway separately.
Come and meet me again at that spot,
Where the horizon meets the heavens.

# मंज़िल से बेखबर

मैं मंज़िलो से बेखबर मांझी
मुखतलिफ़ मझधारों में नाव चलाता रहा
यूं समय रहते हवाओं का रुख पता होता
तो मैं भी सरकशी से किनारे लगा देता


I, a boatman unaware of my destinations,
Kept sailing the boat through various deep currents.
If only I had known the direction of the winds in time,
Then I, too, would have docked it rebelliously at the shore.

# एक हसीन ख्वाब

ये आंखें, इतनी गहरी
कहीं समुंदर तो नहीं?
ये बातें, इतनी हसीं
कहीं तसव्वुर तो नहीं?
मैं ठैरा आशिक
ख्वाबो में रहता हूँ
इतनी कैसे रूहानी?
कोई गहरा स्वपन तो नहीं?

These eyes, so deep,
Are they not perhaps an ocean?
These words, so beautiful,
Are they not just imagination?
I am a dedicated lover,
I live immersed in fantasies.
How can this spiritual purity be real?
Is it not some profound dream?

# प्यार का सफरनामा

लब से, सब से, रब से,
माँगा तुझे बड़ी ज़िल्लत से
मिल जाता तो अच्छा था
अब जो तू ना मिला उतार दिया
दिल से, दिमाग से, ज़ेहन से
तुम होते तो क्या बात-
वरना बीत ही जाती है जिंदगी
मलाल से, खलल से, अमल से

From the lips, from everyone, from God,
I asked for you with great earnestness.
It would have been good if I had found you.
Now that you are not mine, I have removed you—
From the heart, from the mind, from the consciousness.
If you were here, what a wonderful thing it would be—
Otherwise, life just passes anyway,
With regret, with disruption/disturbance, with routine.

# मकान को घर बनाया

तुम तो बोलते थे की
मुझमें तुम्हें अपना घर सा लगता है
तो भला कोई हर बसंत
थोड़े ही अपना घर बदलता है
और मेरे मकान को घर
बनने वाले भी तो तुम ही थे


You used to say that
You felt your own home in me.
Then tell me, does anyone change their own home
Every spring (or every season)?
And you were the one
Who turned my mere structure into a home.

# मफ़रक़त-ए-इश्क़

ये क्या सिला है, मांगा था दिलो का नाता
सीखने को मफ़रकत मिला है
यू में शायर एक दिन में थोड़ी बना हूं
ये मेरा दिल है जो कई बार जला है

What kind of reward is this? I had asked for a bond of hearts,
What I received to learn was parting.
I haven't become a poet in just one day,
This is my heart, which has been burned many times.

# क़ैम इश्क

अब अगली बार आना
तो मौसम सा ना आना
और मौसम सा आना
तो पतझड़ के चंद दिनो सा ना आना
और दिनो सा आना
तो सर्दी के अल्प दिनो सा ना आना
अब आना तो क़ैम आना
लम्हों सा ना आना

Now when you come next time,
Don't come like the weather.
And if you do come like the weather,
Don't come like the few days of autumn/fall.
And if you come like days,
Don't come like the short days of winter.
Now, when you come, come to stay,
Don't come like mere moments.

# अधूरा प्यार

ये कैसा मंज़र दिखाती है जिंदगी
तुझे पा कर भी मैं पा सका नहीं
इस अधूरे प्यार का में क्या करूं
डूबते सूरज सा हर दिन ढलु
तुम रातों में बहुत याद आते हो
इसी खातिर अब सिर्फ दिनों में सोता हूं


What kind of scene does life show me?
Even having you, I could not truly attain you.
What should I do with this incomplete love?
Like the setting sun, I fade away every day.
I remember you intensely throughout the night,
For this very reason, I now only sleep during the daytime.

# ज़ुल्फ़ों का फरमान

दिल गुलिस्तां तू गुलाब
आँखें ज़हर सूरत शबाब
ज़ुल्फ़ों का फरमान कुछ ऐसा शादाब
छूटे शासन बिगड़े नवाब

The heart is a garden, and you are the rose.
Your eyes are poison, your face is youth/beauty.
The decree of your tresses is so fresh and vibrant,
That rulers abandon their reign and nobles lose their composure.

# दिलो की दूरियां

वो साथ मेरे बैठा है
पर किसी और के करीब है
वो अपना सा लगने वाला
किसी और का नसीब है
क्या करूं इस टूटे दिल का
जो मेरा होके भी मेरा रकीब है

He/She is sitting right next to me,
Yet is close to someone else.
That one who feels like my own,
Is the destiny of someone else.
What should I do with this broken heart,
Which, though mine, acts as my own rival?

# रूठा हुआ साया

हवाओं ने कुछ ऐसा रुख मोड़ा है
जो फोन पहली रिंग में उठ जाता था
वो अब घंटो बज के कट जाता है
ये लोग तो वही है
नाजाने क्या नई दूरियां है
मुझसे मुझमें मुज़म्मिल है अब ये मायूसिया
कोई अपना था जो दिल से रूठा है

The winds have taken such a turn,
The phone call that used to be answered on the first ring,
Now rings for hours and is then disconnected.
These people are still the same,
I don't know what these new distances are.
These sorrows are now confined within me.
Someone I considered my own has become estranged.

# किसी और गली

सुना है किसी और गली जाने लगे हो
इसी लिए हमें भुलाने लगे हो?
सोचता हूँ रातो को नींद क्यों नहीं आती
क्यू किसी और के ख्यालों में आने लगे हो?


Rumor has it you're going down a different path now,
Is this why you've started forgetting me?
I often wonder why sleep eludes me at night—
Is it because you've started entering the thoughts of
someone else?

# मिल के भी ना मिला

तेरी एक झलक दिख जाने की ख़ुशी
और सिर्फ एक ही झलक दिख जाने का गम
हार गए तुझे पूरा पाने में भी
और तेरी यादों को भुलाने में हम

The joy of getting just one glimpse of you,
And the sorrow of only getting a single glimpse of you.
I failed both in completely attaining you,
And in forgetting your memories.

# किस्मत का सफर

कुछ रास्ते हमसे ख़फ़ा गए
कुछ मंजिलें भी बेवफा गए
जो लिखा था नसीब में मिलना
वो लफ़्ज़ भी लिखते-लिखते मिटा गए


Some paths became hostile towards me (or avoided me),
Some destinations also turned unfaithful.
The words that were written in destiny for us to meet,
Even those words faded away while being written.

# एक मुलाक़ात

तुझे देखा तो समझा की
ख़ुदा के तर्ज़-ए-क़लम की नईमत क्या है
कुछ लोग मिलते नहीं
बस जिंदगी के तौर पे लिखे जाते हैं


When I saw you, I understood
The true artistry and gift of the Divine Creator.
Some people are not meant to be possessed,
They are simply inscribed as lessons in the book of life

# अक्स-ए-यार

यह हसीन चेहरा और यह लाल चुनर
फ़रामोश हुए मेरे सारे इल्म और हुनर
तू मुझे सिर्फ अपने अक्स से ही साँझा कर
मेरे महबूब लग न जाए तुझे मेरी ही नज़र


So is the beauty of this face and this red veil,
That I have forgotten all my knowledge and skills.
Just share with me only your reflection,
My beloved, may my own gaze not bring you misfortune

www.ingramcontent.com/pod-product-compliance
Lightning Source LLC
Chambersburg PA
CBHW051002030426
42339CB00007B/454